KEYNOTES FOR PILOTS

Maths and Physics for Pilot

Numbers, Signs, Indices and Percentages
Using Symbols
Rules for Solving Algebraic Equations
Triangular Geometry and Trigonometry
Circles
Graphs
Vectors
Aviation Subject Analysis

Dr. Stuart E. Smith

Published by Cranfield Aviation Training School Ltd.

KEYNOTES FOR PILOTS

Maths and Physics for Pilots

British Library Cataloguing in Publication Data.
A catalogue record for this book is available from the British Library.

Previous editions:
ISBN 0-9540275-5-8 (1st edition, 2002) (2nd edition, 2014)

Further volumes in this series are:
Keynotes for Pilots KEYFACTS for EASA PART-FCL PPL examinations 2013/14 (ISBN pending)
Keynotes for Pilots KEYFACTS for EASA ATPL examinations Vol 1 (ISBN pending)
Keynotes for Pilots KEYFACTS for EASA ATP_ examinations Vol 2 (ISBN pending)
Keynotes for Pilots KEYFACTS for EASA ATPL examinations Vol 3 (ISBN pending)

and further publications by Keynotes Aviation Ltd. are:
Vol 1: The JAA CPL (A) Skill Test (ISBN 0-9540275-0-7)
Vol 2: The JAA Instrument Rating (A) Skill Test (ISBN 0-9540275-1-5)
Vol 3: Multi-Crew Co-operation (ISBN 0-9540275-4-X)

Dr. Stuart E. Smith
Published by Cranfield Aviation Training School Ltd.

FOREWORD

Dr. Stuart E. Smith has an acknowledged academic background and trained for his Commercial Pilot Licence (CPL) and Instrument Rating at Oxford, UK. He is currently Head of Training at Cranfield Aviation Training School (a school specialising in Theoretical Knowledge Training for Private, Commercial and Airline Pilots) and is a Private and Commercial Flight Instructor, a FIC Instructor and a PPL Theoretical Knowledge Examiner at Cranfield.

Dr. Stuart E. Smith has collated his extensive experience to provide you with this essential guide for Maths for Pilots.

The Keynotes style with alternating pages of text and space for your personal keynotes relevant to your ground school will ensure that this volume will become a valuable aid to your theoretical knowledge training.

CONTENTS

Introduction

Written to inspire confidence for Pilot training courses from Private to Airline Transport Pilot. The appendices are structured according to the PART-FCL syllabus for the ATPL, each explores the maths and physics associated with the PART-FCL subjects studied at ATPL level offering a collection of the types of problems and their solution in a concise style.

Chapter 1
Numbers, Signs, Indices and Percentages

Whole numbers

A whole number is a number, which is whole, is entire, does not have extra numbers attached to it or is part of a fraction of a whole number. Examples include numbers like: 5, 200, 390 and not numbers like 0.5, 3.142, 200.33 or 390½

Manipulating numbers

There are four fundamental ways of manipulating numbers:

1. Addition
2. Subtraction
3. Multiplication
4. Division

Addition

ADDITION	PLUS	+

Example 1:
Add together 5 and 20

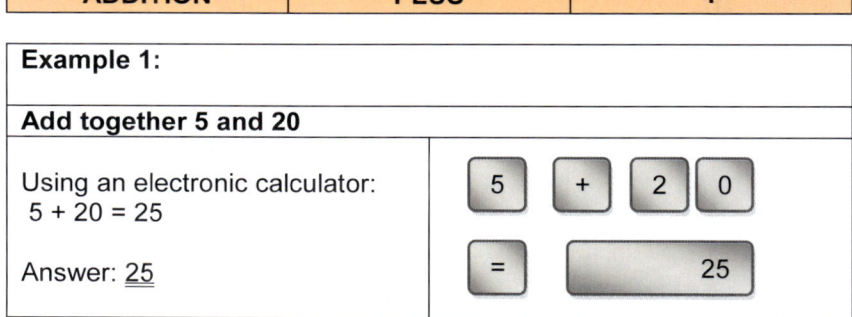

Using an electronic calculator:
5 + 20 = 25

Answer: 25

The order in which the numbers are added up is not important.
For example, 20 + 5 = 25 and 5 + 20 = 25.

Example 2:

Add together 6, 23, 16, 567 and 1256

Using an electronic calculator 6 + 23 + 16 + 567 + 1256 = 1868

Answer: 1868

It is important when doing calculations like that in Example 2 to make a mental check of what the answer could be so that the answer coming out of the calculator makes sense.
To do this, change the numbers into whole numbers that are easy to add up.
For example: 6 is close to 5, 23 is close to 25, 16 is close to 15, 567 is close to 570, and 1256 is close to 1250.
That turns the calculation into 5 + 25 + 15 + 570 + 1250 = 1865
Which means when you see 1868 come out of the calculator then it is likely that you have pressed the correct buttons.

Example 3:

A cross-country flight consists of 3 legs: A to B (81 NM), B to C (66 NM) and C to D (55 NM). (NM = nautical mile)
What is the total distance to be flown?

Using an electronic calculator 81+ 66 + 55 = 202 NM

Answer: 202 NM

Notice the order of addition does not matter.

Example 3 illustrates an important point that only items of the same nature may be added together. If one of the leg distances were given in km and the rest remained in NM then an addition of the numbers would result in an incorrect answer without correcting the units.

Subtraction

SUBTRACTION	MINUS	TAKE AWAY	-

Example 1:

Subtract 40 from 120

Using an electronic calculator
120 − 40 = 80

Answer: <u>80</u>

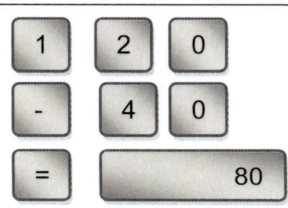

Example 2:

There were 87 kg (kilograms) of screws in storage and 43 kg were sold. How many kg remain?

87 − 43 = 44

Answer: <u>44 kg</u>

As is the case with addition, only 'like' quantities may be subtracted. If there are 8 screws in a bag and 2 are taken away then there are 6 screws remaining. If there are 8 screws and two nails in a bag and 2 nails are taken away then there are 8 screws remaining; only the number of nails is reduced.

Example 3:

Fuel required for an aircraft is 20 lbs for the first leg and 34 lbs for the second leg. If the total on board (excluding adequate reserves) is 200 lbs. How much is expected to be remaining after the trip?

Using an electronic calculator 200 − 20 − 34 = 146 lbs

Answer: <u>146 lbs</u>

Notice the order of subtraction does not matter.

Multiplication

MULTIPLICATION	TIMES	X

To quickly add together a number to itself several times a process called multiplication is used.

Example 1:

In a training school there are 6 classes each with 12 students. Calculate the total number of students.

One method would be addition by adding up 12 to itself 6 times:

Using an electronic calculator 12 + 12 + 12 + 12 + 12 + 12 = 72

A faster method is to multiply:

6 x 12 = 72

Answer: 72 students

Example 2:

What is the total mass of 7 parcels each with a mass of 18 kg?

Using an electronic calculator: 7 x 18 = 126

Answer: 126 kg

Example 3:

For a concrete runway, the landing distance is calculated to be 600 m. On a dry grass runway this distance must be increased by 1.2. What is the required dry grass runway distance?

Using an electronic calculator: 600 x 1.2 = 720 m

Answer: 720 m

Notice the order of multiplication does not matter.

Division

DIVISION	÷	*I*

Division is the process of discovering how many times a number is contained in another number.

Example 1:
If 20 tickets are to be shared by 10 people division provides the answer to the question "How many tickets does each person receive"?
Using an electronic calculator: 20 ÷ 10 = 2 Answer: <u>2 tickets per person</u>

Each person's fraction of the 20 tickets is 2 tickets each.

Example 2:
A load of newspapers weighing 250 kg in total needs to be packed into parcels weighing 50 kg each. How many parcels will there be?
Using an electronic calculator: 250 ÷ 50 = 5 Answer: <u>5 parcels</u>

Example 3:
Part of the process of deriving the maximum Take Off mass is reducing Take Off Distance Available by regulatory factor(s). If Take Off Distance Available is 2200 m and the regulatory factor affecting it is 1.25, what is the de-factored (without the factor) Take Off Distance?
Using an electronic calculator: 2200 ÷ 1.25 = 1760 Answer: <u>1760 m</u>

Brackets

BRACKETS	( )

The purpose of brackets is to group data together. When brackets appear in a calculation the rule is:

DO WHAT IS IN THE BRACKETS FIRST

Example 1:

Calculate: 67 + (23 x 7) – 5

Using an electronic calculator calculate what is in the brackets first:

23 x 7 = 161

Then complete the calculation

67 + 161 – 5 = 223

Answer: 223

It is standard practice to omit the multiplication sign before brackets.

Example 2:

Calculate: 78 + 6 (23 - 12)

78 + 6 (23 - 12) **means** 78 + 6 x (23 –12)

Using an electronic calculator calculate what is in the brackets first:

23 -12 = 11

The 6 belongs to the brackets

6 x 11 = 66

78 + 66 = 144

Answer: 144

The order of using mathematical signs

Consider this sum: 1 + 2 x 3.
It seems simple if you add 1 + 2 you get 3 and if you multiply this by the 3 you get 9.
If you do the multiplication first of 2 x 3 you get 6 and if you add the 1 to this you get 7.
There has to be a rule and this is x and ÷ take priority over + and -.
Most modern scientific calculators follow this rule, but it is important that you know the rule too. The use of brackets, 1 + (2 x 3), simplifies matters, in that you do what it says n the brackets first.

Fractions

Example 1:
Consider a pizza divided into 4 equal parts. How much pizza would each person receive?
Using the division notation this is written as: 1 ÷ 4 or ¼ Answer: <u>¼ of an pizza</u> ¼ + ¼ + ¼ + ¼ = 1 The four quarters of the pizza make a complete pizza

In the fraction ¼ the 1 on the top is known as the numerator and the 4 on the bottom is known as the denominator.

¼ is known as one fourth or a quarter and is known as a proper, common, or vulgar fraction. The larger number is on the bottom.

An improper fraction is one that is 'top heavy' such as 7/3, 4/2 or 8/5.

Manipulation of fractions

As is the case with whole numbers we can only add or subtract 'like' quantities and in this case the lower line (the denominator) defines what we are adding or subtracting.

Adding fractions

Example 1:
What is $\dfrac{1}{4} + \dfrac{5}{8}$?

The problem is to add eighths to quarters.

Eighths and quarters are not 'like' quantities. To add them together they need to have the same denominator. Typically the lowest denominator, which is common to both of them, is chosen.

8 is the lowest common denominator for both of them. For example 8 goes into 8 once and 4 goes into 8 twice.

A quarter is therefore twice the quantity of an eighth i.e. 1 quarter = 2 eighths. 1 / 4 = 2 / 8
Any number of quarters can therefore be converted into eighths by multiplying the numerator (top number) and denominator (bottom number) by 2.

$$\frac{1}{4} \times \frac{2}{2} = \frac{2}{8}$$

(Note that this does not change the value because 2 / 2 is equal to 1)

Using 2 / 8 instead of a 1 / 4 in the original sum results in:

$$\frac{2}{8} + \frac{5}{8} = \frac{7}{8}$$

Answer: 7 / 8

Subtracting fractions

Example 1:

What is $\dfrac{7}{12} - \dfrac{2}{6}$?

The problem is to subtract sixths from twelfths.

Sixths and twelfths are not 'like' quantities. To subtract them from each other they need to have the same denominator. Typically the lowest denominator, which is common to both of them, is chosen.

12 is the lowest common denominator for both of them. For example 12 goes into 12 once and 6 goes into 12 twice.

A sixth is therefore twice the quantity of a twelfth i.e. 1 / 6 = 2 / 12
Any number of sixths can therefore be converted into twelfths by multiplying the numerator (top number) and denominator (bottom number) by 2.

2 / 6 x 2 / 2 = 4 / 12
(Note that this does not change the value because 2 / 2 is equal to 1)

Substituting into the original sum results in:

7 / 12 – 4 / 12 = 3 / 12

3 / 12 may be simplified to 1 / 4

Answer: <u>1 / 4</u>

Multiplying fractions

Example 1:

What is   ¼ x ½ ?

Multiply all the terms above the line together
Multiply all the terms below the line together

1 x 1 = 1
4 x 2 = 8

Answer: 1 / 8

Example 2:

What is   5 / 6 x 7 / 15?

Multiply all the terms above the line together
Multiply all the terms below the line together

5 x 7 = 35
6 x 15 = 90

= 35 / 90

In this example 5 divides into the top and bottom line and is known as a factor of both numbers. This means that the answer can be further simplified as follows:

35 / 5 = 7
90 / 5 = 18

$$\frac{35}{90} = \frac{7}{18}$$

Answer: 7 / 18

Multiples

A multiple is a whole number into which another whole number may exactly be divided into it with no fraction left over.

For example 5 is a multiple of 5 anc 1. In other words, five goes into 5, one time exactly with no fraction left over.

For example 20 is a multiple of 20, 10, 5, 4, 2 and 1. All these numbers go into 20 by exact (whole) amounts with no fractions left over.

Factors

A FACTOR IS A NUMBER WHICH DIVIDES EXACTLY INTO ANOTHER NUMBER

For example 20, 10, 5, 4, 2 and 1 are factors of 20. All these numbers go into 20 by exact (whole) amounts with no fractions left over.

Example 1:
What are the factors of 35?
Answer: <u>1, 5, 7 and 35</u>

Dividing fractions

Example 1:

Calculate $\dfrac{3}{4} \div \dfrac{7}{11}$

Invert the second fraction then multiply the fractions together

$$\dfrac{3}{4} \times \dfrac{11}{7} = \dfrac{33}{28} = 1\dfrac{5}{28}$$

Answer: <u>1 and 5 / 28</u>

Decimal fractions

The fraction $\dfrac{3}{10}$ means 3 tenths and can also be written as 0.3 and in this format is known as a decimal fraction. Decimal fractions relate only to fractions of 10, 100, 1000 etc. All manipulations can be entered immediately into an electronic calculator. Just as the whole number 145 means 1 hundred plus 4 tens plus 5 units so the decimal fraction 0.145 means:

$$\frac{1}{10} + \frac{4}{100} + \frac{5}{1000}$$

Example 1:
How would you write 73 / 100 as a decimal?
Answer: <u>0.73</u>

Example 2:
How would you write 6 / 24 as a decimal?
Using the electronic calculator enter 6 ÷ 24 =
The calculator gives 0.25
Answer: <u>0.25</u>

Adding, subtracting, multiplying and dividing decimals

Unlike working with proper fractions all manipulation can easily be done on the electronic calculator. The rule respecting figures in brackets of course still applies.

Adding fractions

Example 1:
What is $\dfrac{1}{4} + \dfrac{5}{8}$?
Using an electronic calculator: $1 \div 4 = 0.25$ $5 \div 8 = 0.625$ $0.25 + 0.625 = 0.875$ Answer: <u>0.875</u>

Subtracting fractions

Example 1:
What is $\dfrac{7}{12} - \dfrac{2}{6}$?
Using an electronic calculator: $7 \div 12 = 0.58333^{\bullet}$ $2 \div 6 = 0.33333^{\bullet}$ $0.58333^{\bullet} + 0.33333^{\bullet} = 0.91666^{\bullet}$ Answer: <u>0.91666$^{\bullet}$</u> Note: the symbol $^{\bullet}$ means that the number is recurring i.e. the last digit repeats itself for ever.

Multiplying fractions

Example 1:

What is   ¼ x ½ ?

Using an electronic calculator:

$1 \div 4 = 0.25$
$1 \div 2 = 0.5$

$0.25 \times 0.5 = 0.125$

Answer: <u>0.125</u>

Example 2:

What is   5 / 6 x 7 / 15?

Using an electronic calculator:

$5 \div 6 = 0.83333$
$7 \div 15 = 0.46667$

$0.83333 \times 0.46667 = 0.38888$

Answer: <u>0.38888</u>

Dividing fractions

Example 1:
Calculate $\dfrac{3}{4} \div \dfrac{7}{11}$
Using an electronic calculator: $3 \div 4 = 0.75$ $7 \div 11 = 0.63636$ $0.75 \div 0.63636 = 1.1785$ Answer: <u>1.1785</u>

Negative numbers

A negative number is a number less than zero and is denoted with a minus sign.

Manipulating negative numbers

Adding negative numbers

Consider this statement:
If there are 40 nails in a bag and you add -5 nails there will be a total of 35 nails in the bag.

You are adding a negative number, −5 nails!

This is an odd way of saying: If there are 40 nails in a bag and you subtract 5 nails there will be a total of 35 nails in the bag.

40 plus −5 = +<u>35</u>

Example 1:
What is the result if minus 5 is added to 10?
This translates to 10 plus -5 On modern calculators you can type in the numbers and signs in precise sequence, press = and the result is displayed Using an electronic calculator: 10 + -5 = 5 Answer: <u>5</u>

Subtracting negative numbers

Consider this statement:
If there are 40 nails in a bag and you subtract -5 nails there will be a total of 45 nails in the bag.

You are subtracting –5 nails!

This is a very odd way of saying: If there are 40 nails in a bag and you subtract your subtraction of -5 nails there will be a total of 45 nails in the bag. In other words you are adding 5 nails.

40 minus –5 = +<u>45</u>

Example 1:
What is the result if minus 5 is subtracted from 10?
This translates to 10 minus -5 On modern calculators you can type in the numbers and signs in precise sequence, press = and the result is displayed Using an electronic calculator: 10 - -5 = 15 Answer: <u>15</u>

Some rules about signs

Some rules about adding signs follow:

+	and	+	makes a	+
-	and	-	makes a	+
+	and	-	makes a	-
-	and	+	makes a	-

Multiplying negative numbers

This is a short way of adding up a lot of negative numbers.

Example 1:
What is the result if -10 is multiplied by -5?
On modern calculators you can type in the numbers and signs in precise sequence, press = and the result is displayed Using an electronic calculator: -10 x -5 = +50 Answer: <u>50</u>

Dividing negative numbers

Example 1:
What is the result if -10 is divided by -5?
On modern calculators you can type in the numbers and signs in precise sequence, press = and the result is displayed Using an electronic calculator: -10 ÷ -5 = +2 Answer: <u>2</u>

Powers and indices

The expression 10 x 10 is 10 multiplied by itself.

This may be written as 10^2
which is pronounced as 10 to the power of 2

The 2 is known as the index.

Example 1:
How is 10 to the power of 6 expressed?
10 x 10 x 10 x 10 x 10 x10 Answer: $\underline{10^6}$ In this case the 6 is known as the index

Example 2:
What is 3 to the power of 3?
3 x 3 x 3 or 3^3 Answer: $\underline{27}$ In this case the 3 is known as the index

Manipulating numbers with indices

The general rule is that to multiply, the indices are added and to divide the indices are subtracted.

Multiplying numbers with indices

Example 1:
Evaluate $3^4 \times 3^5$
This is equivalent to:
$(3 \times 3 \times 3 \times 3) \times (3 \times 3 \times 3 \times 3 \times 3) = 3^9$
Answer: $\underline{\underline{3^9}}$

Dividing numbers with indices

Example 1:
Evaluate $3^6 \div 3^4$
This is equivalent to:
$(3 \times 3 \times 3 \times 3 \times 3 \times 3) \div (3 \times 3 \times 3 \times 3) = 3^2$
Answer: $\underline{\underline{3^2}}$

Adding numbers with indices

Care needs to be taken when adding numbers with indices. Calculate each component first before adding the results. For example $3^3 + 3^2$ is not the same as $3^3 \times 3^2$.

Example 1:
Evaluate $3^3 + 3^2$

This is equivalent to:

$(3 \times 3 \times 3) + (3 \times 3)$

$27 + 9 = 36$

Answer: <u>36</u>

Square roots

The square root of a number is a smaller number which when multiplied by itself makes the original number. The square root is the opposite of the square of a number.

The square of 3 is displayed as 3^2 which is equivalent to (3 x 3) and is equal to 9.

The square root of 9 is therefore 3.

The symbol for square root is $\sqrt{}$.

Using a calculator $\sqrt{9}$ = <u>3</u>

Example 2:
Find the square root of 81
Using an electronic calculator $\sqrt{81}$ = <u>9</u> Answer: <u>9</u>

Percentages (%)

Percentages are used to express a given quantity based on fractions of 100 (hundredths). To change a fraction into a percentage multiply by 100.

Example 1:
What is 12 / 24 expressed as a percentage
Using an electronic calculator 12 / 24 = 0.5 0.5 x 100 = 50 % Answer: 50%

Example 2:
4 out of 5 examinations are passed at first attempt. What is this pass rate expressed as a percentage?
Using an electronic calculator 4 / 5 = 0.8 0.8 x 100 = 80 % Answer: 80%

Example 3:
The Centre of Gravity an aeroplane is 0.5 m aft of the leading edge of a wing. If the mean aerodynamic chord is 2.5 m what is centre of gravity expressed as a percentage of the mean aerodynamic chord?
Using an electronic calculator 0.5 / 2.5 = 0.2 0.2 x 100 = 20 % Answer: 20%

Manipulating percentages

For a change in percentage the following formula may be used:

> ### THE CHANGE IN THE ORIGINAL QUANTITY X 100%
> ### ORIGINAL QUANTITY

Example 1:

If the price of an airline ticket increases from £75 pounds to £80 what is the percentage increase?

THE CHANGE IN THE ORIGINAL QUANTITY X 100%
ORIGINAL QUANTITY

Using an electronic calculator:

$$\frac{(80 - 75) \times 100\%}{75} \quad = 6.67\ \%$$

Answer: 6.67%

Example 2:

If the price of an airline ticket increases from £80 pounds to £100 what is the percentage increase?

THE CHANGE IN THE ORIGINAL QUANTITY X 100%
ORIGINAL QUANTITY

Using an electronic calculator:

$$\frac{(100 - 80) \times 100\%}{80} \quad = 25\%$$

Answer: 25%

Example 3:

If the price of an airline ticket decreases from £100 pounds to £80 what is the percentage decrease?

$$\underline{\textbf{THE CHANGE IN THE ORIGINAL QUANTITY X 100\%}}$$
$$\textbf{ORIGINAL QUANTITY}$$

Using an electronic calculator:

$$\frac{(100 - 80) \times 100\%}{100} \quad = 20\%$$

Answer: <u>20%</u>

Example 4:

Take-off Distance is calculated to be 3475' for a level concrete runway. This distance should be increased by 5% by each 1% of upslope. If the runway were 1% uphill, what would the new Take-off Distance be?

1% uphill slope means that the calculated Take-off Distance needs to be increased by 5%

5% of 3475' = 5 / 100 x 3475

= 173.75'

The Take-off Distance (TOD) needs to be increased by 173.75'

3475 + 173.75 = 3648.75

Answer = <u>3648.75</u>

A quicker method is to multiply the original TOD by 105%
This is equivalent to multiplying by 105 / 100 or 1.05 / 1.00

3475 x 1.05 = 3648.75

Answer = <u>3648.75</u>

Example 5:

A 125' obstacle is 0.5 NM from the end of the TOD (Take-off distance) what gradient of climb would be required to clear it by 35'?

The percentage gradient required is:

$$\frac{\text{Height change} \times 100}{\text{Horizontal distance}}$$

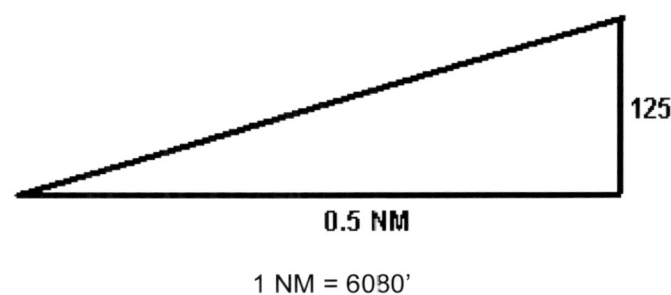

0.5 NM

125

1 NM = 6080'

$$\frac{(125' + 35') \times 100}{0.5 \times 6080'}$$

= 5.26 %

Answer = <u>5.26%</u>

Chapter 2
Using symbols

It is very convenient to use symbols such as letters and then later insert particular numbers to obtain a result. For example:

In a 4 seat aircraft the weight of the pilot is called P and the weight of the passengers A, B and C. The weight of the baggage is X and the fuel F. All weights are in kg.

The total weight of the load is given by:

LOAD = P + A + B + C + X + F

> **THE STATEMENT LOAD = P+A+B+C+X+F IS KNOWN AS A FORMULA**

On a particular flight the pilot weighs 76 kg, passenger A, 56 kg passenger B, 87 kg, there is no one sitting on seat C. The baggage is 35 kg and the fuel on board is 85 kg. What is the load?

Load = P + A + B + C + X + F = 76 + 56 + 87 + 0 + 35 + 85 = 339 kg

Answer: Load is 339 kg

Example 1:

Using the formula A = B + C

where B = 7 and C = 34 find A

A = B + C
A = 7 + 34
A = 41

Answer: A = 41

Example 2:

Using the formula A = 5(B + C) / 7

where B = 3 and C = 21 find A

Do what is in the brackets first

B + C = 3 + 21 = 24

A = 5 x 24 / 7 = 17.14

Answer: <u>17.14</u>

In addition to the English alphabet, Greek letters are often used such as α (alpha), β (beta) and ρ (rho). These symbols are manipulated in the same way as English symbols. One very special Greek letter is π (pi) which always takes a particular value (3.142 to three decimal places) and represents the circumference of any circle divided by its diameter.

Consider the equation:

$\beta = 12 + 7$

The answer is 19 and in this case β is the subject of the equation. Suppose a formula is presented as:

$3 + \beta = 13$

In this case β is not the subject of the equation. By inspection β must be 10 for the two sides to balance.
Consider a more complex formula:

$23 + 50\beta = 1023$

In this case the solution is not immediately obvious and the best method is to make β the subject of the equation i.e. to make β appear on its own on the top to the left of the equals sign. The rule when manipulating equations is:

Whatever is done to one side of an equation must be done to the other

In the equation if 23 is subtracted from the left hand side this leaves 50β but to obey the rule, 23 must also be subtracted from the right hand side.

$23 + 50\beta - 23 = 1023 - 23$

Therefore: $50\beta = 1000$

In order to isolate β on the top left hand side. Both sides must be divided by 50.

$$\frac{50\beta}{50} = \frac{1000}{50}$$

$$\beta = \frac{1000}{50} = 20$$

Example:

Given the equation 57B − 125 = 875

solve for B

Solution

Add 125 to each side giving:

57B − 125 + 125 = 875 + 125

57B = 1000

Divide both sides by 57

B = 1000 / 57 = 17.54

Using indices with symbols

$B \times B = B^2$

$B \times B \times B = B^3$

$B^2 \times B^3 = B^5$

Multiplying out brackets

$(M + 5)(M + 7) = M^2 + 12M + 35$

Explanation

$(M + 5)(M + 7)$ means $(M + 5) \times (M + 7)$

Everything in the first bracket must be multiplied by everything in the second

First multiply the M in the first bracket by the M and the 7 in the second

$M \times M = M^2$
$M \times 7 = 7M$

Next multiply the 5 in the first bracket by the M and the 7 in the second

5 x M = 5M
5 x 7 = 35

Putting all the terms in one line gives:

M^2 + 7M + 5M + 35 and adding together the 7M and the 5M terms simplifies the expression to:

$\underline{M^2 + 12M + 35}$

Chapter 3
Rules for Solving Algebraic Equations

Algebra is a branch of mathematics that uses letters to represent numbers

A *formula* is a mathematical rule expressed algebraically, that is, using letters to represent related quantities. Many formulae take the form of an *equation*, in which two expressions are made equal to each other

In algebra, a *term* is a collection of numbers, letters and brackets, all multiplied or divided together

Terms are separated by + and − signs, for example, in the expression

$$4xy + 5x^2 - 2y + 6y^2 + 4$$

there is an xy term, an x^2 term, a y term, a y^2 term and a numerical term.

When different letters are multiplied together they are just written next to each other, usually in alphabetical order, for example, xy means x multiplied by y.

x multiplied by x is written as x^2.

At the front of the expression there is an invisible + sign preceding the xy term.

Solving an equation means finding the value or values of the terms for which the equation is true. The *solution* to an equation is said to 'satisfy' the equation

To assist in its solution, an equation may be rearranged, or *transposed*. In transposing an equation, as shown in Chapter 2 whatever is done to one side must also be done to the other

An equation may be transposed to make one term the *subject* of the equation, that is, defining it in relation to all the other terms. For example, in the equation:

$f = c / \lambda$

f is defined in terms of c and λ, making f the subject.

Transpose to make λ the subject

Multiply both sides by λ:

$\lambda f = \lambda c / \lambda$

On the right hand λ / λ cancels out to give 1.0 leaving:

$\lambda f = c$

Divide both sides by f to give:

$\lambda f / f = c / f$

On the left hand side f / f cancels out to give 1.0 leaving:

$\underline{\lambda = c / f}$

It is convenient to simplify equations by collecting 'like' terms

For example, in the expression:

$2x - 4 + 5x + 6$

each term, including its preceding + or -, may be isolated then moved into a preferred order, so that 'like' terms are together:

$+2x + 5x + 6 - 4$

This then simplifies to

$7x + 2$

Before it is possible to collect 'like' terms it may be necessary to multiply out brackets

The term outside a bracket multiplies each separate term inside the bracket, for example:

$3(2y) = 3 \times 2 \times y = 6y$

The following rules apply when multiplying signs:

+	times a	+	makes	+
-	times a	-	makes	+
-	times a	+	makes	-
+	times a	-	makes	-

Where a *fraction* is expressed algebraically, the rules are the same as for ordinary fractions

When multiplying two algebraic fractions, multiply top and bottom separately and cancel if possible.

When dividing two algebraic fractions, invert the second fraction then multiply top and bottom separately and cancel if possible.

When adding or subtracting two algebraic fractions, derive a *common denominator*, that is, a 'same' bottom line and then add the top lines only.

Most equations can be solved by step by step manipulation
All steps obey the rule that what is done to one side must be done to the other

Exercise:

1. $F = ma$

i. Given $F = 735$ N and $a = 9.8$ m/s^2, find m
ii. Given $F = 640$ N and $m = 80$ kg, find a

2. $\dfrac{P_1 V_1}{T_1} = \dfrac{P_2 V_2}{T_2}$

i. Given $P_1 = 1013.25$ hPa, $V_1 = 10$ l, $T_1 = 288$ K, $P_2 = 506$ hPa and $T_2 = 252$ K, find V_2

3. $PV = nRT$

i. Given $P = 2026.5$ hPa, $V = 0.5$ l, $n = 1$ and $T = 121.86597$ K, find R
ii. Given $P = 1.013$ x 10^4 hPa, $V = 1.0$ l, $n = 2$ and $R = 8.314462$, find T

4. Mach number $= \dfrac{TAS}{LSS}$

i. Given LSS $= 38.94\sqrt{T}$, $T = 208$ K and Mach number $= 0.74$, find TAS

5. Lift $= c_L qS$

i. Given $q = \frac{1}{2}\rho v^2$, $c_L = 0.5$, $\rho = 1.225$ kg/m^3, $v = 200$ m/s and $S = 500$ m^2, find Lift
ii. Given $q = \frac{1}{2}\rho v^2$, $c_L = 0.5$, $\rho = 1.225$ kg/m^3, Lift $= 2$ x 10^5 N and $S = 250$ m^2, find v
iii. Given $q = \frac{1}{2}\rho v^2$, Lift $= 25\,000$ N, $\rho = 1.225$ kg/m^3, $v = 200$ m/s and $S = 250$ m^2, find c_L

Answers:
1. i) 75 kg, ii) 8 m/s^2
2. i) 17.5 l
3. i) 8.314462, ii) 609.18 K
4. i) 416 KT
5. i) 6125000, ii) 51 m/s, iii) 0.004

Chapter 4
Triangular Geometry and Trigonometry

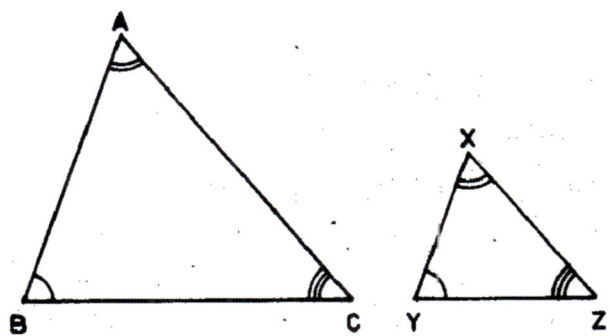

Fig. 4.1 Similar triangles

Two triangles are said to be *similar* if their angles are the same. If two triangles are similar their *corresponding sides*, meaning the sides opposite the equal angles, are proportional.

The triangles in Figure 4.1 are similar triangles since, taking the angles A, B and C and X, Y and Z,

A = X
B = Y
C = Z

Also,

$$\frac{\text{side AB}}{\text{side BC}} = \frac{\text{side XY}}{\text{side YZ}}$$

> The sum of the internal angles of any triangle is 180°

> **In a right-angled triangle one of the angles is equal to 90°. The side opposite the right-angle is the longest and is called the hypotenuse**

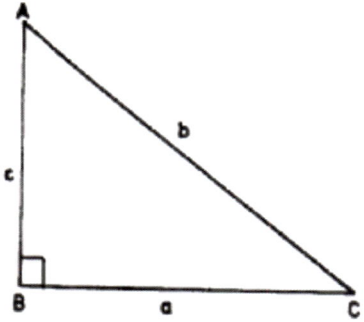

Figure 4.2 A right-angled triangle

Pythagoras theorem states that in a right-angled triangle, the square of the hypotenuse is equal to the sum of the squares of the other two sides

In Figure 4.2

$$b^2 = a^2 + c^2$$

For example in the triangle in figure 4.2:

If side a = 3 and c = 4

then b^2 = 9 + 16 = 25

Thus <u>b = 5</u>

Example 2:

If DME slant range = b, height = c and plan range = a and the following values for slant range are 10 NM and height are 6000' (1 NM) then what is the plan range?

$b^2 = a^2 + c^2$

slant range^2 = plan range^2 + height^2

10^2 = plan range^2 + 1^2
100 = plan range^2 + 1
99 = plan range^2
plan range = $\sqrt{99}$
plan range = 9.95 NM

Trigonometry

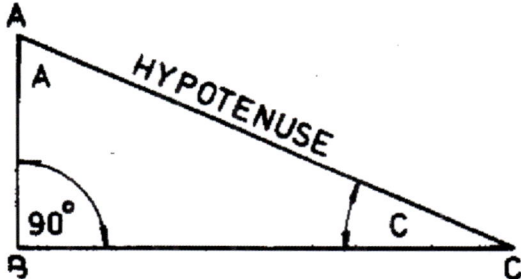

Figure 4.3 Taking the angle C in the right-angled triangle shown, the side of the triangle adjacent to C, side BC, is called the adjacent side and the side opposite the angle C, side AB, is called the opposite side. The longest side is called the hypotenuse

Sine cosine and tangent (often abbreviated sin, cos and tan) represent the ratios of the length one side of a triangle to the length of another side

The sine of an angle $= \dfrac{\text{length of opposite side}}{\text{length of hypotenuse}}$

The cosine of an angle $= \dfrac{\text{length of adjacent side}}{\text{length of hypotenuse}}$

The tangent of an angle $= \dfrac{\text{length of opposite side}}{\text{length of adjacent side}}$

40

50

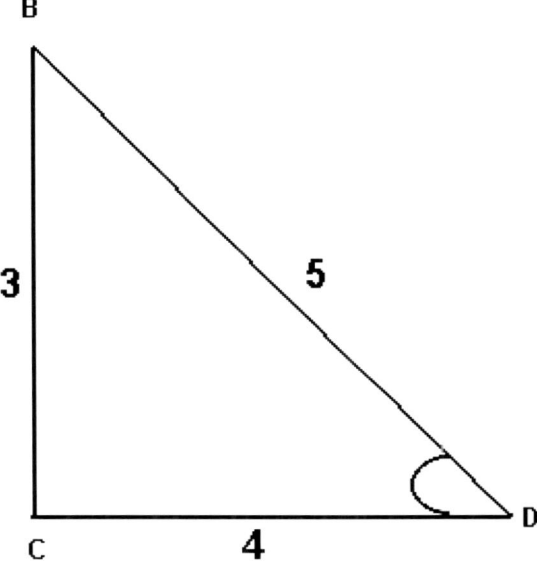

Figure. 4.4

In figure 4.4:

Sin D = 3 / 5 = 0.6

Using the $\sin^{-1}$ function on the calculator

D = $\sin^{-1}$ 0.6

Therefore

D = 36.87°

Using cos D = 4 / 5 or tan D = 3 / 4 will give the same result.

Chapter 5
Circles

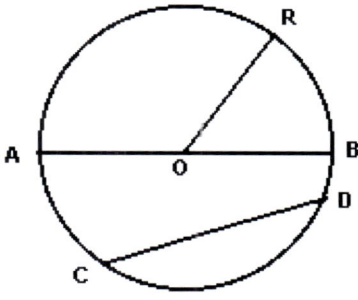

Figure 5.1

In the circle shown in figure 5.1 the line AB is a diameter, O is the centre, OR is a radius and CD is a chord.

By convention the radius is normally depicted by the letter r and because OA and OB are also radii then the diameter is equal to 2r.

Diameter = 2 x radius

The total distance round the edge of the circle is called the circumference and is described by the formula:

Circumference = 2 π r

The Greek letter π is a mathematical constant and is approximately equal to 3.142 and is found on most electronic calculators.

Area = π r²

There are 360° in a circle

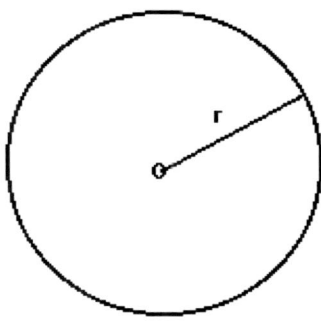

Figure 5.2

In figure 5.2 if the radius r = 23.2 km calculate the diameter, the circumference and the area of the circle.

The diameter = 2r = 2 x 23.2 = <u>46.4 km</u>

The circumference = 2πr = 2 x π x 23.2 = <u>145.8 km</u>

The area = $πr^2$ = π x 23.2^2 = <u>1690.9 km^2</u>

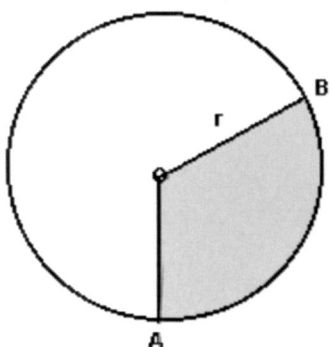

Figure 5.3 Sectors

In figure 5.3 if the angle AOB is 120° and the radius is 23.2 km what is the area of the shaded sector?

The area of the whole circle from the previous calculation is 1690.9 km^2 and there are 360° in a circle so the area of the shaded sector is:

120 / 360 X 1690.9 = <u>563.6 km^2</u>

In figure 5.3 if the angle AOB is 120° and the radius is 23.2 km what is the length of the arc of the circumference AB?

The circumference of the whole circle is 145.8 km as calculated above so the length of the arc AB is

120 / 360 x 145.8 = <u>48.6 km</u>

Chapter 6
Graphs

Data in either a table or graphical form. Graphs often convey the information more readily than words or tables and for this reason are widely used in aviation.

Suppose the speed of an aircraft V varies with the time (t) according to the equation:

$V = 10 + 5t$

This can be depicted on a graph as follows:

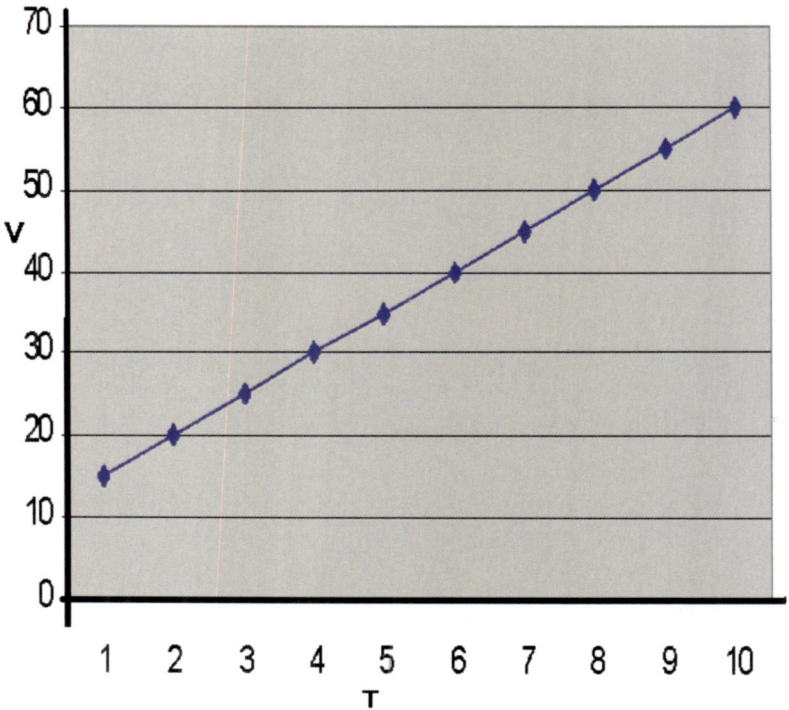

Figure 6.1

It is conventional for the vertical axis to be known as the y-axis and the horizontal the x-axis.

The intersection of the two axes (position O) is known as the point of origin.

To obtain the graph in figure 6.1 for the equation V = 10 + 5t values of V are plotted for several values of t and these are then joined.

Once the graph is plotted values of V for any value of t can immediately be read directly from the graph.

<u>For example when t = 6, V = 40.</u>

The graph in figure 6.1 is a straight line and any equation which does not have an x^2 or higher index will always be a straight line.

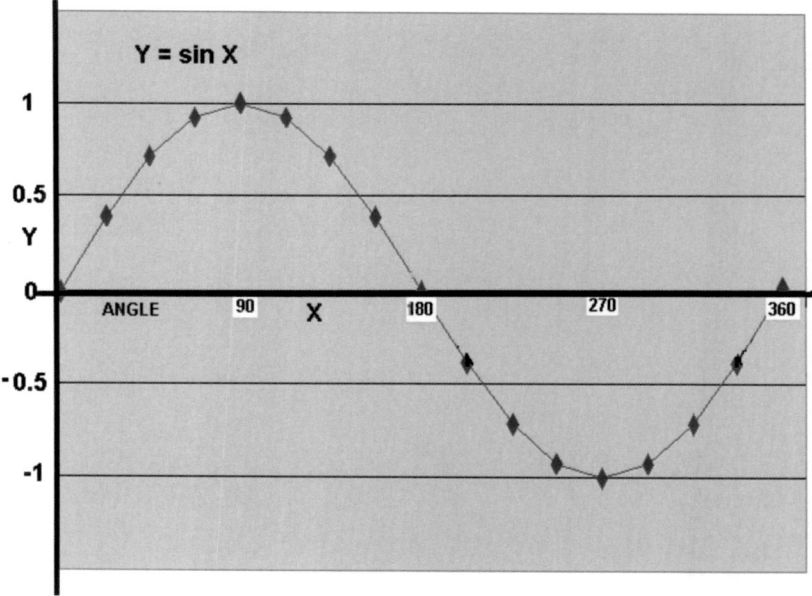

Figure 6.2

In contrast to the straight line graph figure in 6.1 the graph in figure 6.2 depicts the equation:

<u>y = sin x</u>

And is plotted for values of the angle x from 0° to 360°.

Chapter 7

Vectors

A vector is a quantity that possesses both size (magnitude) and direction

A velocity, for example, requires both magnitude and direction to describe it and hence is a vector quantity. Speed is not a vector quantity since when one refers to a speed of 40 KT no direction is implied. Such a quantity is called a *scalar*.

Any vector can be represented by a straight line, the length of the line representing the magnitude and the direction of the line representing the direction of the vector

An aircraft in flight has two velocities, the first being its velocity through the air and the second its velocity along the ground. A third vector, the wind, determines how one relates to the other and makes up a *triangle of velocities*.

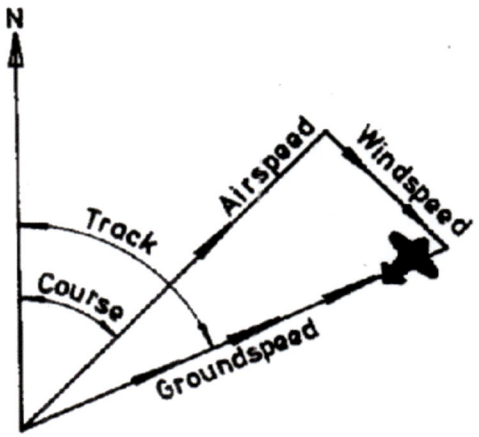

Figure 8.1 With a slight tailwind, the vector representing the aircraft's groundspeed is larger than that representing its airspeed

Example:

At 10.00 h an aeroplane departs aerodrome P to fly to aerodrome Q which is 250 km away along track 055°. The wind is 30 kph from 300° and the aeroplane's true airspeed is 200 kph. What heading should the pilot steer and what is the aeroplane's estimated time of arrival?

From the triangle of velocities heading is 047° and groundspeed is 219 kph, thus the time taken to fly 250 km is:

$$\frac{250}{219} = 1 \text{ h } 8 \text{ min}$$

Thus the estimated time of arrival is 11.08 h

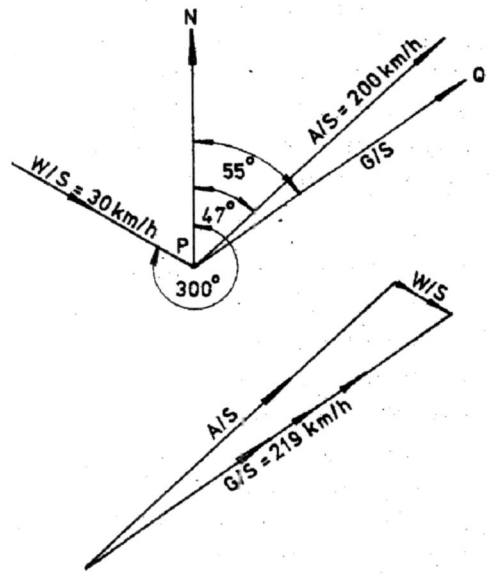

APPENDICES
SUBJECT ANALYSIS

There are 14 ATPL examinations:

Air Law & ATC Procedures.
Aircraft General Knowledge: Airframe / Systems / Electrics /
Powerplant and Emergency Equipment
Flight Planning & Monitoring
General Navigation
Human Performance & Limitations
IFR Communications
Instrumentation
Mass and Balance
Meteorology
Operational Procedures
Performance
Principles of Flight
Radio Navigation
VFR Communications

There are 13 CPL examinations with IFR Communications being
omitted from the ATPL set and subject content is reduced.

The mathematical elements in these examination subjects are in the
following appendices. Reference should be made to the earlier parts of
this book if problems are encountered in completing calculations.

Appendix 1
Air Law & ATC Procedures

1.1 SI Units

ICAO Annex 5 to the Convention on International Civil Aviation '*Units of Measurement to be Used in Air and Ground Operations*', states that:

'*The International System of Units (SI Units) shall be used as the standard system of units of measurement for all aspects of international civil aviation air and ground operations*'

The name SI derives from 'Système International d'Unités'. The system has evolved from units of length and mass (metre and kilogram) created by the Paris Academy of Sciences and adopted by the French National Assembly in 1795. The original system became known as the metric system.

An advantage of SI is that there is only one unit for each physical quantity. From these base units, units for all other mechanical quantities are derived. Some of these derived names have special names, for example the Newton (N) is the unit for the product of mass and acceleration, i.e. for force.

Annex 5 permits the use of particular non-SI units including the tonne (t), degree (°), degree Celsius (°C), minute (min), hour (h), day (d), week, month and year. Due to their widespread use and to avoid potential safety problems, Annex 5 also permits the use of the nautical mile (NM), foot (') and knot (KT).

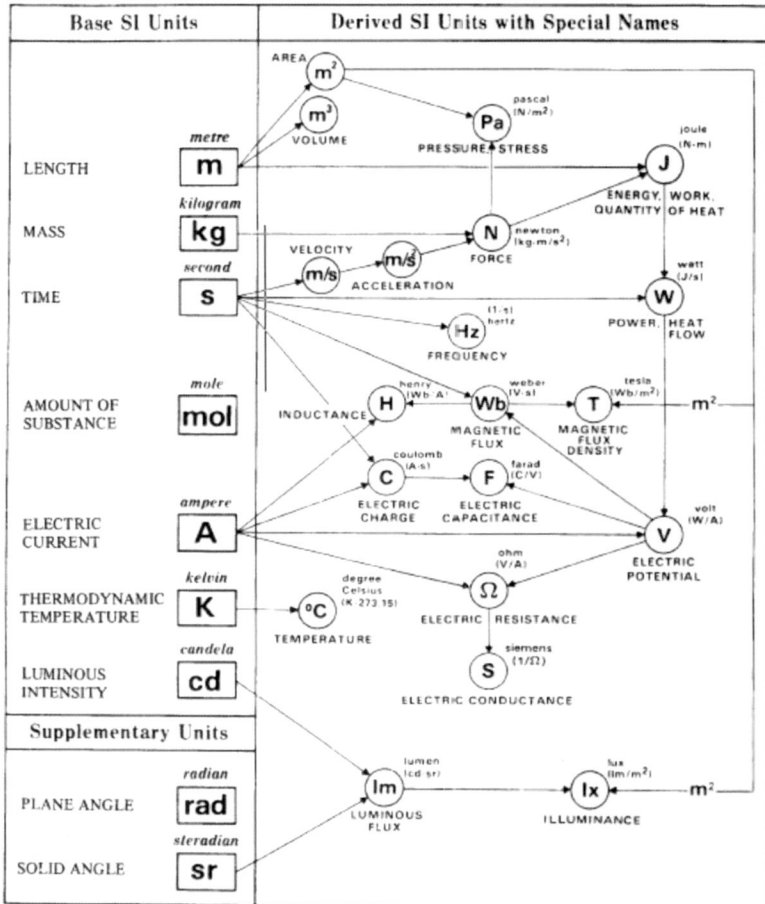

Figure 1.1 Base SI Units and Derived SI Units with Special Names
(ICAO Annex 5)

Multiplication factor	Prefix	Symbol
1 000 000 000 000 000 000 = 10^{18}	exa	E
1 000 000 000 000 000 = 10^{15}	peta	P
1 000 000 000 000 = 10^{12}	tera	T
1 000 000 000 = 10^{9}	giga	G
1 000 000 = 10^{6}	mega	M
1 000 = 10^{3}	kilo	k
100 = 10^{2}	hecto	h
10 = 10^{1}	deca	da
0.1 = 10^{-1}	deci	d
0.01 = 10^{-2}	centi	c
0.001 = 10^{-3}	milli	m
0.000 001 = 10^{-6}	micro	μ
0.000 000 001 = 10^{-9}	nano	n
0.000 000 000 001 = 10^{-12}	pico	p
0.000 000 000 000 001 = 10^{-15}	femto	f
0.000 000 000 000 000 001 = 10^{-18}	atto	a

Table 1.1 SI Unit prefixes (ICAO Annex 5)

1.2 Errors and Accuracy

There are two types of error to consider:

A measurement error always exists when a physical quantity is measured

Example:

ICAO Document 8168 Aircraft Operations (Part III Paragraph 2.2.3) explains that the accuracy of the dimensions of fixes used in instrument approach procedures is influenced by factors such as ground station tolerance, airborne receiving system tolerance, flight technical tolerance and distance from the facility.

Therefore, the accuracies of facilities providing track are given as:

VOR	± 5.2°
ILS localiser	± 2.4°
NDB	± 6.9°

These are examples of *measurement error* in which, for a VOR track say, the actual track could be anywhere between the measured track plus or minus 5.2°.

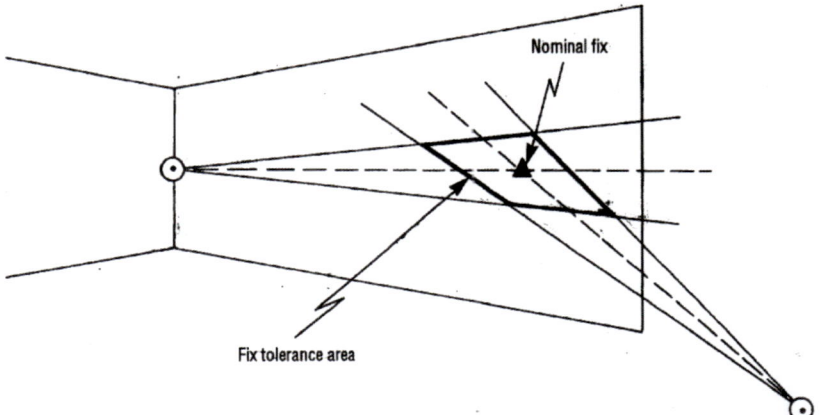

Figure 1.2 Intersection fix tolerance area – an example of measurement error (ICAO Doc 8168 Figure III-2-2)

A rounding error is present when a number is rounded to a specific number of decimal places (d.p.) or significant figures (s.f.)

Rounding errors also arise as a calculator or computer truncates numbers with which it is working or displaying.

Example

ICAO Annex 2 *Rules of the Air* (Table 3.1) states that

'*Above 900 m (3000 ft) AMSL or above 300 m (1000 ft) above terrain, whichever is the higher, VMC minima are 1500 m horizontally and 300 m (1000 ft) vertically*'

If, more accurately, it is assumed that 1 m is equal to 3.281 feet, i.e. a *conversion factor* of 3.281, 900 m is equal to 2952.9 ft, correct to one decimal place, and 300 m is equal to 984.3 ft, correct to the same number of decimal places. The 3000 ft and 1000 ft quoted in Annex 2 are examples of *rounding errors*.

Appendix 2
Aircraft General Knowledge

What is the formula for aquaplaning speed?

Vp (KT) = 9 x √tyre pressure (PSI)

How are Impedance, Voltage and Current related?

$$\text{Impedance (Z)} = \frac{Voltage\ (V)}{Current\ (I)}$$

What is the formula for total capacitance in series?

$$\frac{1}{C_T} = \frac{1}{C_1} + \frac{1}{C_2} \cdots$$

What is the formula for total capacitance in parallel?

$$C_T = C_1 + C_2 \cdots$$

What is the formula for total resistance in series?

$$R_T = R_1 + R_2 \cdots$$

What is the formula for total resistance in parallel?

$$\frac{1}{R_T} = \frac{1}{R_1} + \frac{1}{R_2} \cdots$$

What is the short formula for only two resistances in parallel?

$$R_T = \frac{R_1 \times R_2}{R_1 + R_2}$$

How is generator frequency calculated?

$$Generator\ Frequency\ (Hz) \quad = \quad \frac{Rotor\ rpm \times No.\ of\ pole\ pairs}{60}$$

In an AC system what is apparent power?

Apparent power (KVA) = Voltage x Current

In an AC system what is real power?

Real power (KW) = apparent power x power (cos Φ)

What is the formula for force?

Force = mass x acceleration

What is the formula for power?

Power (watts) = force x TAS

What is the formula for engine power?

Engine power = shaft torque x rpm

What is the formula for thrust power?

Thrust power = thrust x TAS

What is the formula for propulsive efficiency?

$$Pr\,opulsive\ efficiency \quad = \quad \frac{Thrust\ (horse)\ power}{Brake\ (horse)\ power}$$

What is the formula for compression ratio?

$$Compression\ ratio \quad = \quad \frac{Total\ Volume}{Clearance\ Volume}$$

How are manifold and boost pressure converted?

1 PSI $\approx$ 2 inches of Hg
e.g.   Manifold 45 inches of Hg $\approx$ 7.5 PSI boost
45 – 29.92 $\approx$ 15 inches of Hg excess

$$\frac{15}{2} \ = \ 7.5 \ PSI \ boost$$

What is bypass ratio?

$$Bypass \ ratio \ = \ \frac{Cold \ bypass \ air}{Hot \ core \ air}$$

What is pressure ratio?

$$Pressure \ ratio \ = \ \frac{Outlet}{Inlet}$$

What is engine pressure ratio?

$$EPR \ = \ \frac{Downstream \ of \ turbine}{Inlet}$$

Appendix 3
Flight Performance & Planning

What is the formula for Nautical Ground Miles?

$$NGM = \frac{NAM \times GS}{TAS}$$

What is the formula for Nautical Air Miles?

$$NAM = \frac{NGM \times TAS}{GS}$$

What is the formula for Specific Air Range?

$$SAR = \frac{Range\ in\ Still\ Air\ (NM)}{Fuel\ Burnt\ (kg)}$$

What is the formula for Gross Fuel Flow?

$$GFF = \frac{Fuel\ Burnt\ (kg)}{Range\ in\ Still\ Air\ (NM)}$$

What is the formula for Point of Equal Time?

$$PET = \frac{D \times H}{O + H}$$

What is the formula for Point of Safe Return?

$$PSR = \frac{E \times O \times H}{O + H}$$

Appendix 4
General Navigation

CONVERGENCY = CHANGE IN LONGITUDE x SINE OF MEAN LATITUDE

CONVERSION ANGLE = CONVERGENCY / 2

EXAMPLE: Find the value of convergency and conversion angle between N35 00 E028 25 and N32 30 W015 30.

Method:

First find the mean (average) latitude by adding the two latitudes and dividing by 2

N35 00 + N32 30 = N67 30
(67 30) / 2 = 33 45

Change in longitude (chlong) is the difference between E028 25 and W015 30
As the longitudes are in different hemispheres they must be added to obtain the difference.

028 25 + 015 30 = 43 55

Putting these figures into the convergency equation and using a scientific calculator:

Convergency = 43 55 x sin 33 45 = 24°

Conversion angle = 24 / 2 = 12°

CONVERTING LONGITUDE (ARC) INTO TIME

EXAMPLE:

Calculate the time taken for the Sun to travel from Greenwich EW000 00 to W060 00

METHOD:
The Sun travels 360° in 24 h which is a mean velocity of 15° of longitude per h.
From EW000 to W060 the change in longitude (chlong) is 60°.

Time taken = 60 / 15 = 4 h

CONVERTING TRUE HEADING TO MAGNETIC HEADING

VARIATION WEST MAGNETIC BEST
VARIATION EAST MAGNETIC LEAST

EXAMPLE:

True heading is 105 T variation is 5 W. What is the magnetic heading?

METHOD:

Variation is west so compass is 'best' i.e. the most

105 + 5 = 110 M

Magnetic heading = 110

CONVERTING MAGNETIC HEADING TO COMPASS HEADING

DEVIATION WEST COMPASS BEST
DEVIATION EAST COMPASS LEAST

EXAMPLE:

Magnetic heading is 110 M deviation is 2 E. What is the compass heading?

METHOD:

Deviation is east so compass is 'least'

110 - 2 = 108 C

Compass heading = 108 C

CALCULATING RECIPROCALS

ADD OR SUBTRACT 180

The reciprocal of a direction is the reverse (opposite) direction.

EXAMPLE: Calculate the reciprocal of 093.

093 + 180 = reciprocal = 273

Another method of doing this without the need for a calculator is to add 200 and subtract 20 (or subtract 200 and add 20).

093 plus 200 is 293
293 minus 20 is 273

Relative bearings

A relative bearing is a bearing measured with respect to the nose of the aircraft, i.e. to the aircraft heading. While the actual geographical direction of a bearing (in degrees true) does not change when an aircraft changes heading, the presentation of the bearing on certain equipment, such as the ADF (Automatic Direction Finder) will change, relative to the nose of the aircraft as features outside the window relative to your viewpoint.

Relative bearings are converted into true bearings by adding true heading and converting into the reciprocal if need be to be able to plot from a known ground feature.

EXAMPLE : An aircraft is heading 040T and obtains an ADF bearing of a radio station of 080° relative. Calculate the bearing of the aircraft from the radio station.

RULE : Relative bearings are converted to true bearings by adding true heading.

Relative bearing	080 R
True heading	<u>040T</u>
True bearing	120T

120T - This is the bearing of the radio station from the aircraft, which has to be converted into the bearing of the aircraft from the station.

True bearing of station from the aircraft	120T
Reciprocal	<u>+180°</u>
True bearing of aircraft from the station	300T

A bearing of 300T would be plotted from the station to the aircraft.

Converting grid to true and vice versa

Convergency East - True Track least
Convergency West - True Track best

EXAMPLE 1
Northern hemisphere: the track is 123 Grid and convergency is 18°W, calculate true track.

Track   123 G
Convergency   18 +

"Convergency west, true track best"

Track   141 T best

EXAMPLE 2
Northern hemisphere: The heading is 105G or 095T, calculate convergency.
"Convergency east, true track least."

Heading   105 G
Heading   095 T
Convergency   10 E

Magnetism

Calculate the values of Z and T for a position where dip is 65° and the value of H is 0.2 units.

METHOD
Tan dip = Z / H
Z = H tan 65
Z = 0.43

Coefficient B = $\dfrac{\text{deviation on east - deviation on west}}{2}$ = $\dfrac{E - W.}{2}$

Coefficient C = $\dfrac{\text{deviation on north - deviation on south}}{2}$ = $\dfrac{N - S.}{2}$

Deviation is the result of coefficients A, B and C. To find deviation on any heading all three coefficients must be known.
Coefficient A is constant on all headings. Coefficient B varies as sine of the heading. Coefficient C varies as cosine of the heading.

FORMULA:
Deviation on any heading = A + B sin hdg + C cos hdg

Example 1:
A compass has Coefficients A = +1; B = +2: C = +3. Calculate the deviation on headings 045 and 225
Deviation on 045C = +1   + 2 sin 045   + 3 cos 045
= +1+1.41 +2.12   = +4.53 (total deviation).
Deviation on 225C = +1   +2 sin 225   +3 cos 225   =
    +1 -1.41 -2.12   = -2.53 (total deviation).

Example 2:
Coefficient A on a compass is +2 and B is +3. Total deviation on heading 230C is -4°. Calculate the value of coefficient C.

Dev on 230C = +2 + 3 sin 230 + C cos 230
-4   = +2 -2.3 + C cos 230
-3.7 = C cos 230

C = 5.75

Scale

Scale = Chart length
        Earth distance

EXAMPLE 1
When one inch equals 20 NM, express the scale of the chart as a representative fraction.

METHOD 2
Use the formula and convert all values to the same units.

Scale = Chart length ÷ Earth distance = 1" / (20 NM x 6080' x 12")

Substitution gives 1 : 1 459 200 as the representative fraction.

EXAMPLE 3
Chart scale is 1 : 1 000 000. Calculate the number of NM on the Earth shown by 2 inches on the chart.

Scale = CL ÷ ED, so $\frac{1}{1\,000\,000}$ = $\frac{2}{ED}$ ".   So, ED = 2 000 000".

Convert to NM.
2 000 000" = 27.41 NM

CALCULATION OF SCALE AT DIFFERENT LATITUDES

When the scale at one latitude on a Mercator chart is known, the scale at any other latitude may be calculated by a formula:

Scale Denominator A x cosine B = Scale denominator B x cosine A

where A and B are the latitudes.
NOTE : A or B may be either latitude.

EXAMPLE 1

Scale at the Equator on a Mercator chart is 1 : 2 000 000, calculate the scale at S 40.

METHOD

Let A be the equator and B S40.

ABBA

Scale denom. A x cos B		=	Scale denom B x cos A
2 000 000	x cos 40	=	Scale denom B x cos 0.

So that Scale denom B = 2 000 000 x cos 40
The scale denominator of latitude "B" is therefore 1 532 089.
The scale at S 40 is therefore 1 : 1 532 089.

Departure

Departure = dlong x cosine mean latitude

EXAMPLE 1
Calculate the rhumb line track & distance from S4720 E02930 to S4720 E01615.

METHOD

The two positions are on the same parallel – S47 20. Therefore, they lie east / west of each other (090 degrees / 270 degrees T). They are also on the rhumb line track 090 degrees / 270 degrees T. The distance between them can be calculated by means of the departure formula:

Departure = ch long x cos lat

The ch long is E29 30 – E16 15 = 13 15 = 795 minutes of longitude (required by the formula).

So, departure (NM) = 795 cos 47 20 = <u>539 NM</u>.

In-flight navigation

EXAMPLE 1
Calculate the still air distance travelled at 275 KTAS for 35 min.

275 x 0:35 = 160 air nautical miles (NAM).

EXAMPLE 2
Calculate the ground nautical miles flown at a groundspeed of 545 KT for 1 h 13 min.

545 x 1:13 = 663 ground nautical miles (NGM).

TAS calculation

An alternative method of calculating TAS from RAS which gives an approximate result is by using the formula:

TAS = RAS + (1.75% RAS per 1000 ft msl)

EXAMPLE
Calculate the approximate TAS in the standard atmosphere at 150 KT RAS at FL100.

1.75% x 10 = 17.5%
150 KT + 17.5% = 176 KT

Calculation of maximum range

METHOD
Maximum range is equal to endurance multiplied by groundspeed.

EXAMPLE
Calculate the maximum range of an aircraft for the following conditions:

- True air speed 450 KT
- Wind component + 65 KT
- Fuel flow 4550 kg/h
- Usable fuel 29120 kg

Endurance = $\dfrac{\text{Usable fuel}}{\text{Fuel flow}}$ = $\dfrac{29120}{4550}$ = 6.4 i.e. 6:24.

GS = 515 KT. 515 x 6:24 = 3296 NM.

Point of Safe return (PSR)

Distance to the PSR = $\dfrac{\text{(Endurance)(GSO)(GSH)}}{\text{(GSH) + (GSO)}}$ or $\dfrac{\text{E x O x H}}{\text{O + H}}$

where:

- E = endurance in hours and minutes
- GSO or O = groundspeed on to destination in KT
- GSH or H = groundspeed home (or back or return) to departure in KT.

EXAMPLE
Calculate the distance to the point of safe return for the following circumstances:

- An aircraft has a total fuel load of 6400 kg.
- The average fuel flow is 800 kg/h.
- Reserves of 800 kg are kept
- TAS is 250 KT
- The wind component outbound is +50 KT
- The wind component for the return is -50 KT.

METHOD
Fuel on board is 6400
Reserves are 800
Fuel for the flight is 5600
Endurance = 5600/800 = 7 h
GSO is 250 + 50 = 300 KT
GSH is 250 − 50 = 200 KT
Substitution in the formula gives : $\dfrac{7 \times 300 \times 200}{500}$ =   840 NM

Point of Equal Time

The formula for calculating the distance to the PET is:

Distance to the PET
  = $\dfrac{\text{Total Distance x Groundspeed Home}}{\text{Ground Speed On + Ground Speed Home}}$ or $\dfrac{D \times H}{O + H}$

where :
- •   D is total distance
- •   GSO or O = groundspeed on to destination in KT
- •   GSH or H = groundspeed home (or back or return) to departure in KT

EXAMPLE
Calculate the distance to the PET and ETA for the following data:

- •   Total distance from departure to destination is 1000 NM
- •   ATD 1345Z
- •   250 KTAS
- •   Wind component from departure to destination 50 KT HW
- •   Wind component back to departure 30 KT tailwind.

METHOD
By substitution in the formula : $\dfrac{1000 \times 280}{200 + 280}$ = 583 NM

Density Altitude

Density Altitude = Pressure altitude + (120' x ISA deviation)

Rate of climb / Gradient Calculations

EXAMPLE

Calculate the rate of climb for a climb gradient of 3.5 % and a groundspeed of 120 KT.

Gradient x $\dfrac{\text{distance in one minute}}{100}$ = rate of climb

$\dfrac{3.5 \times 2 \times 6080'}{100}$ = rate of climb = 426 fpm

Appendix 5
Human Performance & Limitations

What is the formula for Body Mass Index?

$$BMI = \frac{Weight\ (kg)}{Height\ (m)^2}$$

What is the BMI of a pilot of mass 84 kg and height 5' 10"?

5' x 12" = 60"
60" + 10" = 70"
70" x 2.52 = 177.8 cm = 1.778 m

$$BMI = \frac{84}{1.778^2}$$

BMI = <u>26.6</u>

Appendix 6
IFR Communications

What is the formula for maximum theoretical range?

$$MTR \;=\; 1.23 \times \left[\sqrt{Ht\ Tx} \;+\; \sqrt{Ht\ Rx} \right]$$

What is the relationship between frequency and wavelength?

$$F \;=\; \frac{c}{\lambda}$$

What is the relationship between aerial height and wavelength?

$$\text{Aerial height} \;=\; \frac{\lambda}{2}$$

Appendix 7
Instrumentation

What is the formula for calculating CAS?

$$CAS = 1/2 \, \rho \, V^2$$

What is the formula to calculate the Local Speed of Sound?

$$LSS = 38.94 \times \sqrt{T \text{ (Kelvin)}}$$

What is the formula to calculate Mach Number?

$$MN = \frac{TAS}{LSS}$$

What is the formula for Earth Rate?

$$ER = 15 \sin lat$$

(Decreasing in Northern hemisphere)

What is the formula for Latitude Nut?

$$LN = 15 \sin lat$$

(Increasing in Northern hemisphere)

What are the formulae for Transport Wander?

$$TW = dlong \times \sin lat$$

$$TW = \frac{GS}{60} \times \tan lat \times \cos \theta \text{ (EW angle)}$$

Appendix 8
Mass and Balance

What are the fuel conversions?

kg	x 2.2	=	lbs
Imp Gallons	x 1.205	=	US Gallons
US Gallons	x 3.784	=	Litres
litres	x S.G.	=	kg

What is the floor loading equation?

$$\text{Pallet size} = \frac{\text{Load}}{\text{Floor Loading}}$$

What is the formula for expressing the Centre of Gravity as a percentage of Mean Aerodynamic Chord?

$$\text{MAC (\%)} = \frac{CG - LE}{MAC} \quad x \quad 100$$

What is the formula for CG position from datum?

$$\text{CG position from datum} = \frac{\text{Total Moment}}{\text{Total Mass}}$$

What is the formula for finding the mass to be moved to put the C of G within limits?

$$\text{Mass to be moved} = \frac{\text{Total Aircraft Mass x Distance to move CG}}{\text{Distance Load is Moved}}$$

Appendix 9
Meteorology

What is Charles' Law?

$$T \propto V$$

What is Boyle's Law?

$$P \propto \frac{1}{V}$$

How is pressure related to density and temperature?

$$P \propto D \times T$$

What does Geostrophic wind depend upon?

$$V = \frac{PGF}{2\,\omega\,\rho\,\sin\,lat}$$

How do you calculate ISA temperature?

Convert the pressure altitude to FL	eg. 25000' = FL250
Knock off a zero	25
Double it	50
Put a minus sign in front	-50
Add 15	-35

What is the formula for calculating true altitude when temperature differs from ISA?

$$\% \; Altitude \; Correction = \frac{ISA \; deviation}{2.5}$$

.

Appendix 10
Operational Procedures

What is the formula for aquaplaning speed?

Vp (KT) = 9 x √tyre pressure (PSI)

Appendix 11
Performance

How is Runway Slope calculated?

$$\text{Runway Slope} = \frac{\text{Difference in threshold elevations}}{\text{Shortest TORA}} \times 100$$

What is the formula for gradient of climb?

$$\text{Gradient of climb} = \frac{\text{Thrust} - \text{Drag}}{\text{Weight}} \times 100$$

Appendix 12
Principles of Flight

Lift

$$L = C_L \tfrac{1}{2} \rho V^2 S$$

where $\tfrac{1}{2} \rho V^2$ = dynamic pressure
C_L = lift coefficient

Drag (Profile)

$$D = C_D \tfrac{1}{2} \rho V^2 S$$

where C_D = drag coefficient

Induced Drag

$$C_{Di} = \frac{k C_L^2}{\pi A}$$

where C_{Di} = induced drag coefficient

C_L = lift coefficient
A = aspect ratio
k = induced drag factor (equals 1 for elliptical lift distribution)

therefore C_{Di} is proportional to C_L^2

Relation between weight and stalling speed

$$V_S \text{ (new weight)} = V_S \text{ (old weight)} \sqrt{\frac{\text{new weight}}{\text{old weight}}}$$

Load factor in a turn

$$n = \frac{1}{\cos \phi}$$

where ϕ = angle of bank

Relation between stalling speed and load factor (n)

$$V_S (n) = V_S (1g) \sqrt{n}$$

Effect of gusts on the load factor (given increase in C_L due to a gust)

Load factor (n) in a gust: $n_{new} = n_{old} \left(\dfrac{C_{Lnew}}{C_{Lold}} \right)$

where C_{Lnew} = old C_L + C_L increase

Stalling speed in a turn

$$V_S \text{ (turn)} = V_S \text{ (1g)} \sqrt{\frac{1}{\cos \phi}}$$

where ϕ = angle of bank

Calculation of stalling speed as bank angle changes

$$V_S \text{ (new } \phi) = V_S \text{ (old } \phi) \sqrt{\frac{\cos \text{ (old } \phi)}{\cos \text{ (new } \phi)}}$$

Design manoeuvre speed

$$V_A = V_S \text{ (1g)} \sqrt{\text{limiting } n}$$

Calculation of V_A following change in weight

$$V_A \text{ (new weight)} = V_A \text{ (old weight)} \sqrt{\frac{\text{new weight}}{\text{old weight}}}$$

Radius of turn

$$r = \frac{V^2}{g \tan \phi} \text{ metres}$$

where $g = 9.81 \text{ m/s}^2$

V = speed in m/s
ϕ = angle of bank

Rate of turn

$$\text{rate} = \frac{g \tan \phi}{V} \text{ radians / s} \qquad \text{where} \quad g = 9.81 \text{ m / s}^2$$

$$V = \text{speed in m/s}$$
$$\phi = \text{angle of bank}$$

1 radian = 57.3°

$$\text{rate of turn in degrees / s} = 57.3 \frac{g \tan \phi}{V}$$

Note: rate of turn and radius of turn are NOT affected by weight, only by speed and angle of bank

Appendix 13
Radio Navigation

What is the formula for maximum theoretical range?

$$MTR = 1.23 \times \left[\sqrt{Ht\ Tx} + \sqrt{Ht\ Rx} \right]$$

What is the other formula for maximum theoretical range?

$$MTR = \frac{c}{2\ PRF}$$

What is the formula relating PI and PRF?

$$PRF = \frac{1}{PI}$$

What is the relationship between frequency and wavelength?

$$F = \frac{c}{\lambda}$$

What is the conversion factor from KT to m/s?

$$m/s = \frac{KT}{1.944}$$

How is Optimum Usable Frequency calculated?

Optimum Usable Frequency = 85% of Maximum Usable Frequency

How do you calculate range on a DME?

$$DME\ Range\ (NM) = \frac{161800\ NM/s \times (time - 50\ \mu s)}{2}$$

How do you calculate slant range on a DME?

$$\text{Slant Range}^2 \quad = \quad \text{Plan Range}^2 + \text{Height}^2$$

How is the height on descent on the ILS calculated?

$$\text{Height (feet)} \quad = \quad \text{Glide slope angle} \times 100 \times \text{dis}\tan\text{ce NM}(+50')$$

How is the Rate of Descent on the ILS calculated?

$$\text{ROD (fpm)} \quad = \quad \frac{\text{Glide slope angle} \times 100 \times \text{Ground Speed}}{6\text{C}}$$

For an NDB how is range of the ground wave affected by power over land?

$$Range\,(NM) \quad = \quad 2 \times \sqrt{Power\,(W)}$$

For an NDB how is range of the ground wave affected by power over sea?

$$Range\,(NM) \quad = \quad 3 \times \sqrt{Power\,(W)}$$

Appendix 14
VFR Communications

What is the formula for maximum theoretical range?

$$MTR = 1.23 \times \left[\sqrt{Ht\ Tx} + \sqrt{Ht\ Rx} \right]$$

$$MTR = 12 \times \sqrt{FL}$$

What is the relationship between frequency and wavelength?

$$F = \frac{c}{\lambda}$$

What is the relationship between aerial height and wavelength?

$$\text{Aerial height} = \frac{\lambda}{2}$$